PRESIDENTIAL SUC[illegible]
IN EGYPT [illegible]
ON U.S.-EGYPTIA[illegible]

INTRODUCTION

Egypt is a critical cc[illegible] the U.S. military and strategic interests. Its location—straddling the African and Asian continents on the west-to-east air corridor route to the oil-rich Persian Gulf region, possessing the important Suez Canal waterway, and next door to the volatile Israeli/Palestinian situation—make it a vital partner for the United States. In addition, as the most populous country in the Arab world, and home to long-standing centers of learning in the Muslim world, what happens in Egypt is often a bellwether for developments in other parts of the region. Perhaps not surprisingly, President Barack Obama chose Egypt as the venue to deliver a major outreach speech to the Muslim world in June 2009.

Ever since the late President Anwar Sadat switched sides in the Cold War in the 1970s, Egypt has been a valuable, though sometimes prickly, partner of the United States, assisting it with military and political support, especially during times of crisis, as in the first Gulf War of 1990-91. A glimpse of some of this support was made public in 2006 when the U.S. Government Accounting Office, in a report to Congress, revealed that between 2001 and 2005, Egypt provided over-flight permission to 36,553 U.S. military aircraft and granted expedited transit of 861 U.S. naval ships through the Suez Canal.[1] Since the late 1970s, U.S. military assistance to Egypt has held steady at $1.3 billion a year, much of it for Cairo's purchase of U.S. weapons and other military equipment. It is estimated that this assistance comprises about 80 percent of Egypt's military procurement budget. U.S. military aid, as well as joint training exercises, most notably the biennial Bright Star, have helped to foster close military ties, including efforts to achieve interoperability of forces.[2]

President Sadat's successor, Hosni Mubarak, when in power, oversaw this cooperation from the Egyptian side since 1981. A former air force commander, Mubarak carefully nurtured close U.S.-Egyptian strategic ties because he saw them as being in Egypt's national interests, even when the two countries did not see eye-to-eye on some important political issues, like the Iraq War of 2003. Mubarak also maintained the Egyptian-Israeli peace treaty despite several flare-ups and small wars that have occurred between Israel and some of its neighbors between 1982 and 2006, which inflamed public opinion inside Egypt. Maintaining relations with Israel, even though it has been characterized as a "cold peace," has diminished the possibility of a general Arab-Israeli war which otherwise could jeopardize vital U.S. interests in the region.

President Mubarak ruled Egypt in an authoritarian manner, similar to that of his predecessors, Anwar Sadat and Gamal Abdel Nasser. Although he allowed some political dissent as well as independent media outlets, the general authoritarian nature of the Egyptian regime has not changed fundamentally since the Free Officer coup or revolution of 1952. Under Mubarak, presidential power was overwhelming, backed by strong military and security establishments, with parliament as a weak institution. In contrast to his predecessors, however, Mubarak refused to appoint a vice president. The reasons for this unwillingness was the subject of much speculation inside Egypt, and may have had to do with his concern that such

External Research Associates Program Monograph

PRESIDENTIAL SUCCESSION SCENARIOS IN EGYPT AND THEIR IMPACT ON U.S.-EGYPTIAN STRATEGIC RELATIONS

Gregory Aftandilian

September 2011

*****

Comments pertaining to this report are invited and should be forwarded to: Director, Strategic Studies Institute, U.S. Army War College, 632 Wright Ave, Carlisle, PA 17013-5046.

*****

This manuscript was funded by the U.S. Army War College External Research Associates Program. Information on this program is available on our website, *www.StrategicStudiesInstitute.army.mil*, at the Publishing button.

*****

All Strategic Studies Institute (SSI) publications may be downloaded free of charge from the SSI website. Hard copies of this report may also be obtained free of charge while supplies last by placing an order on the SSI website. The SSI website address is: *www.StrategicStudiesInstitute.army.mil*.

*****

The Strategic Studies Institute publishes a monthly e-mail newsletter to update the national security community on the research of our analysts, recent and forthcoming publications, and upcoming conferences sponsored by the Institute. Each newsletter also provides a strategic commentary by one of our research analysts. If you are interested in receiving this newsletter, please subscribe on the SSI website at *www.StrategicStudiesInstitute.army.mil/newsletter/*.

ISBN 1-58487-506-2

FOREWORD

The momentous events in Egypt since January 25, 2011, have focused the world's attention on that critical country. Mostly young, pro-democracy activists appear to have successfully challenged Egypt's authoritarian government and its long-time leader. President Hosni Mubarak has been driven from office and is reportedly in poor health. Hence, regime change is virtually certain. The Egyptian military, long a major power broker, gained popular support for its restrained reaction to the uprisings of January-February 2011 and currently (July 2011) the Supreme Council of the Armed Forces, headed by Field Marshall Hussein Tantawi, leads the nation pending promised elections in the autumn. However, recent events suggest that the military may be reluctant to relinquish power fully, and popular unrest against it is rising. Thus, most scenarios discussed in this paper, or variations thereof, are still very possible.

Egypt has been a close ally of the United States since the late 1970s when the late President Anwar Sadat changed sides in the Cold War and embarked on a peace process with Israel that led to the Camp David Accords in 1978 and the Egyptian-Israeli peace treaty in 1979. In return, Egypt became one of the largest recipients of U.S. aid, receiving $1.3 billion in military assistance, plus substantial amounts of civilian assistance each year. Since that time, the Egyptian military has developed close ties with their U.S. counterparts, exemplified by joint military exercises, the training of Egyptian officers in U.S. military schools, and Egypt's purchases of U.S. military equipment. This close military-to-military cooperation has assisted U.S. strategic objectives in the volatile Middle East region, with the United States receiving expedited transit for its naval ships through the Suez Canal as well as overflight rights for U.S. military aircraft. In addition, the Egyptian and U.S. Governments cooperate closely on anti-terrorism issues. Suffice it to say that the United States has relied on Egypt for strategic cooperation for more than 3 decades, including vital assistance on Arab-Israeli peace process issues.

Prior to the events of January 25, 2011, most of the attention on Egypt was focused on the presidential succession issue, given that President Mubarak had achieved an advanced age, had several medical operations that put his health in doubt, and had steadfastly refused to appoint a vice president. There was also widespread speculation that he was grooming his son, Gamal Mubarak, to succeed him despite rumors that the Egyptian military establishment had strong doubts about Gamal's qualifications, in part because he had not done military service. Although the developments of January and February 2011 seemed to have overtaken events as they were known in 2010, the issue of presidential succession remains both highly relevant and timely. Whatever type of successor government comes to power in Egypt, it is likely that, given Egyptian history, the post-Mubarak president will have strong powers (though probably not to the extent of President Mubarak), to include remaining the head of the Egyptian military establishment.

Gregory Aftandilian, a consultant, academic, and a former State Department Egypt analyst, wrote this monograph for the U.S. Army War College as part of its External Associates Program, which encourages scholars to write studies on critical, strategic issues facing the United States in different regions of the world. He completed this study in December 2010, prior to the outbreak of pro-democracy demonstrations in Egypt the following month. In this monograph, he clearly examines Egypt's partnership with the United States, its importance to U.S. strategic objectives in the region, the power structure in Egypt, and several possible presidential succession scenarios. He also examines how each of these scenarios would impact U.S. strategic relations with Egypt, and gives clear recommendations for U.S. policymakers.

Although some of the scenarios outlined in this monograph are no longer viable—for example, it is hard to conceive that Mubarak would be able to move back into power, and highly unlikely that his son, Gamal Murarak, would be a presidential contender—other scenarios remain plausible, particularly given what we see as the more prominent role of the Egyptian military in this fluid political situation. In addition, some of the possible presidential successors that Aftandilian mentions have now risen to higher positions in the Egyptian government. Aftandilian also discusses the sensitive issue of the Muslim Brotherhood, Egypt's most organized opposition group that is opposed to many U.S. policies. He examines a scenario of a Muslim Brotherhood-dominated government, but notes that this is unlikely to occur unless both the Brotherhood and the Egyptian military split apart.

We hope this study will be of assistance to U.S. policymakers as they deal with a critical ally during a very sensitive and tumultuous period.

DOUGLAS C. LOVELACE, JR.
Director
Strategic Studies Institute

ABOUT THE AUTHOR

GREGORY AFTANDILIAN is an independent consultant, writer, and lecturer, having spent over 21 years in government service, most recently on Capitol Hill. He was foreign policy advisor to Congressman Chris Van Hollen (2007-08), professional staff member of the Senate Foreign Relations Committee and foreign policy adviser to Senator Paul Sarbanes (2000-04), and foreign policy fellow to Senator Edward Kennedy (1999). Prior to these positions, Mr. Aftandilian worked for 13 years as a Middle East analyst at the U.S. Department of State where he was a recipient of the Department's Superior Honor Award for his analyses on Egypt. His other government experiences include analytical work for the U.S. Department of Defense and the Library of Congress. He was also a research fellow at the Kennedy School of Government at Harvard University (2006-07) and an International Affairs Fellow at the Council on Foreign Relations in New York (1991-92). In addition, Mr. Aftandilian has worked as a consultant on Egyptian affairs for the National Democratic Institute for International Affairs, and is an adjunct faculty member at Boston University and Northeastern University. Mr. Aftandilian is the author of *Egypt's Bid for Arab Leadership: Implications for U.S. Policy* (1993); and *Looking Forward: An Integrated Strategy for Supporting Democracy and Human Rights in Egypt* (2009). Mr. Aftandilian holds a B.A. in history from Dartmouth College, an M.A. in Middle Eastern studies from the University of Chicago, and an M.S. in international relations from the London School of Economics.

SUMMARY

Although this monograph was written before the pro-democracy demonstrations in Egypt in January 2011, it examines the important question as to who might succeed President Hosni Mubarak by analyzing several possible scenarios and what they would mean for U.S. strategic relations with Egypt. The monograph first describes the importance of Egypt in the Middle East region and gives an overview of the U.S.-Egyptian strategic relationship. It then examines the power structure in Egypt to include the presidency, the military, and the ruling party. The monograph next explores various succession scenarios. Although some of these scenarios have been overtaken by events because President Mubarak has been driven from office and his son, Gamal Mubarak, is no longer a viable candidate given the popular anger against the Mubarak family, the other scenarios are still plausible. Scenarios envisioning a short-term take-over by Omar Soliman, Ahmed Shafiq, or other members of the current or former military establishment would likely preserve U.S strategic interests, provided such take-overs are of short duration and result in a transition to democratic civilian rule. However, if the military does not return to the barracks, then U.S.-Egyptian strategic relations would be adversely affected because it is unlikely that the U.S. Congress and the U.S. administration would continue to provide aid to what would be a military dictatorship. An immediate transition to a civilian president, such as opposition leader Mohammad El-Baradei or former foreign minister Amre Moussa would not adversely affect the substance of the overall U.S.-Egyptian relationship because both are establishment figures, though the United States should expect some distancing by either one of them in the bilateral relationship over some U.S. policies in the region. The worst-case scenario for the United States would be a Muslim Brotherhood-dominated government, but for this to occur, both the Brotherhood and the Egyptian military would each have to split, with radical elements collaborating to form a new government; this is not a very likely scenario. During a presidential succession period, U.S. policymakers should understand that the transition will happen based on events and processes inside of Egypt, not those in Washington. U.S. officials should avoid backing a particular Egyptian presidential candidate and instead speak about adherence to the rule of law and the Egyptian Constitution. In the case of a military take-over, even one of short duration, U.S. officials should emphasize the need to return to civilian rule as soon as possible.

a person might overshadow him. Regardless, given Mubarak's advanced age (82 years old), and persistent health problems (he had several major medical operations in Europe in the past few years),[3] the question of presidential succession loomed large over the Egyptian political horizon. Even now, after Mubaraks' overthrow, this succession could have profound implications for U.S.-Egyptian strategic relations. This monograph addresses various succession scenarios in Egypt and speculates on how they will impact strategic ties between our two countries. It will also provide policy recommendations of how U.S. officials should conduct themselves during what will likely be a very sensitive and potentially volatile period in Egypt's political development.

THE POWER STRUCTURE IN EGYPT

Egypt's political system has been described as "authoritarian" and indeed, "pharoanic."[4] In 1952, a group of military officers from middle class and lower middle class backgrounds, called the "Free Officers," without a clear ideology except for nationalism and anti-imperialism, staged a coup against the unpopular monarch. Soon after, they dissolved the monarchy and political parties and established a military-dominated regime with a charismatic military officer, Gamal Abdel Nasser, at its helm. Nasser embarked on a socialist economic policy, replete with an expansion of the bureaucracy and nationalization of industries. Although he later became a civilian prime minister and president, Nasser relied heavily on his fellow military officers to become members of his cabinet, administrators of the nationalized businesses, and even ambassadors to foreign countries.[5] The social transformation was profound. By 1965, the public sector accounted for 95 percent of all investment and controlled 85 percent of production, while the bureaucracy increased by 161 percent in size between 1961 and 1971. As one scholar put it: "Socially, the regime set out to transform Egyptian society."[6] Nationalization of businesses and land reform policies destroyed the old commercial and land-owning elite. Political and economic changes "created their own dynamic and allowed the regime to depend on a new lower middle class composed of peasants, clerks, small bureaucrats, teachers, nurses, etc."[7] But throughout this transformation under Nasser, "the Egyptian military was there to protect the regime and participate in governing."[8] Most of the cabinets between 1952 and 1970 were controlled and dominated by the military. Nasser created a political organization to support this system, first called the Liberation Rally and later the Arab Socialist Union, but these institutions were clearly subordinate to the president and the military. Indeed, in 1962, for example, about three-fourths of the General Secretariat of the Arab Socialist Union were military officers.[9] Up until his death, Nasser was the unrivaled leader of this authoritarian and praetorian system.

The military's role in governing declined under Nasser's successor, Anwar Sadat, himself one of the Free Officers. Although Sadat, like Nasser, used the military as a base of power, he feared certain centers of power within the military establishment and purged and reshuffled many officers until he made the military "subordinate to the civilianized leadership of the president" that resulted in a "more professional military dedicated to external defense."[10] Sadat's decision in 1973 to embark on a surprise attack on Israeli forces in the Sinai, which was lost in Egypt's disastrous 1967 war against Israel, boosted his reputation at home, as did later peace overtures to Israel which, while initially controversial, eventually led to direct U.S. involvement in the peace process, the Camp David Accords, the subsequent Egyptian-Israeli peace treaty (which led to the restoration of Egyptian sovereignty over the Sinai), and an economically beneficial relationship with the United States. In the economic sphere, Sadat pursued a more free enterprise economic program, characterized by an open-door policy of attracting foreign investment, and he even allowed some former members of the rural elite to reclaim their confiscated lands. Under Sadat a new economic elite emerged who were tied to the regime, often cited as an example of "crony capitalism." Politically, Sadat transformed the Arab Socialist Union into the National Democratic Party and allowed some other parties to emerge, but he did not want the parliament to dominate the system. Toward the end of his rule (and shortly before his assassination), Sadat became increasingly dictatorial, arresting hundreds of his opponents as well as his former allies. It should also be noted that while the military's role in the political system declined under Sadat, and he relied on a younger generation of officers, notably the leaders of the 1973 war, to head the military establishment, he was compelled to rely on the military to restore order when widespread riots broke out in January 1977 over food price rises and the police were unable to put down the riots.[11]

Sadat's vice president at the time of his assassination was Hosni Mubarak, the former air force commander and a hero of the 1973 war. After surviving the shock of the assassination (the assassins were radical Islamists in the military) and putting down a related uprising in Upper Egypt, Mubarak liberalized the political system somewhat to boost his own legitimacy. In late 1981, he freed most of the political prisoners who were arrested under Sadat's orders and allowed fairly free parliamentary elections to take place in 1984. On the economic front, he pursued a gradual economic liberalization policy, lifting subsidies on certain commodities in a slow and deliberate manner and downsizing (through early retirements) and privatizing a number of state-own industries. Like Sadat, Mubarak also had to rely on the military to put down a major domestic crisis—the 1986 riots by poorly-paid conscripts in the Central Security Forces who had heard a false rumor that their length of service would be extended from 2 to 3 years.[12]

The military under Mubarak has played even less of a role in governing than it did under Sadat. Indeed, in the current cabinet, outside of the Defense Minister, there is only one former high-ranking military officer, Ahmed Shafiq, head of the civil aviation ministry. Military officers have been content to serve under a civilian president (though himself a former career military officer) because Mubarak has allowed them to maintain their autonomy, perquisites, and economic interests.

In addition to serving the national defense, Egypt's military establishment today can be described as a vast economic conglomerate. It has control over various industries ranging from the production of armaments to washing machines and pharmaceuticals, and is nearly self-sufficient in agriculture. It has even branched into such sectors as "road and housing construction, consumer goods, and resort management."[13] One scholar has estimated that the military's economic activity contributes $500 million of Egypt's gross domestic product (GDP).[14] Although in theory the military's budget is subject to parliamentary review,

> . . . no actual oversight ever takes place. Egypt's minister of defense makes an annual presentation to the assembly's standing committee on Defense, National Security, and Mobilization and is obliged to answer parliamentary questions, but such questions are rare. As one military informant explained, 'The minister of defense may brief the parliament but there is no real dialogue, the members are not culturally inclined to question the military'.[15]

Although the pay of a military officer is not high, it is generally better than that of civilian civil servants of equivalent rank, and the military has access to special food stores, hospitals, vacation condominiums, and foreign travel that are denied to other members of the bureaucracy. In retirement, many military officers become high-paid consultants for the defense industries and foreign firms, managers of defense plants, and appointees of governorships and other state institutions.

Because the Egyptian military (with the exception of the 1967 war debacle) has a positive reputation as the defender of Egypt's national sovereignty, has a large force level (believed to be around 400,000)[16] and depends on conscription, it is generally well-regarded by the population. Moreover, as one scholar has explained, Egyptian citizens do not resent the benefits given to the military because each family has, at one time or another, at least one member serving in it.[17]

The other center of power in Egypt is what has been called the "businessmen-politicians" — those members of the ruling National Democratic party who have risen to prominence under the president's son, Gamal Mubarak, a deputy leader of the party who was also head of the party's powerful Policies Secretariat.[18] Gamal and his businessmen allies used their positions to remove socialist language from the Constitution (passed by a referendum), liberalize foreign trade, and make Egypt more business-friendly. However, these policies did not level the economic playing field, as some of these businessmen-politician have retained their strangleholds on certain industries. Ahmed Ezz, whose company has a monopoly on steel imports to Egypt, is chairman of the parliament's planning and budgetary committee, while Mohammed Abu El-Enein, chairman of the private sector Cleopatra Group, is the chairman of parliament's committee for industry and energy.[19] These and other businessmen, some analysts say, not only went into politics to make sure that their businesses were protected, but to ensure that they themselves would not be arrested on corruption charges, as parliamentary members are generally immune from prosecution.

While Gamal and his businessmen allies represented the so-called "new-guard" in the party, the so-called "old guard"—those who began their political careers under the old Arab Socialist Union—are still around but in lesser numbers and with less influence. Nonetheless, the old guard has not been entirely sidelined, until the recent rebellion they had allies in the bureaucracy and among those in the party who were opposed to Gamal Mubarak.

As for the opposition, the largest and most important group is the Muslim Brotherhood, which had been hampered by regime policies. Persecuted by Nasser, the Brotherhood was allowed to resurface under Sadat, but neither he, nor his successor, Hosni Mubarak, gave it legal status. Mubarak initially was tolerant of the Brotherhood, which developed an extensive social-welfare apparatus (alleviating some economic burdens of the state), but when the Brotherhood's reach extended to traditional institutions (winning control of the Bar Association in 1992 as well as other professional syndicates and university faculty clubs), the regime moved against it.[20] Moreover, in the 1990s when Egypt was racked by violent attacks by more extremist elements, such as those by the Egyptian Islamic Jihad and the Islamic Group, the Mubarak government sought to lump all Islamist groups together (even though there was no evidence that the Brotherhood took part in this violence), arrested a number of Brotherhood second-echelon leaders, and prosecuted them before special military courts which were established to handle terrorism cases. For reasons that will be explained later in this monograph, the Brotherhood rebounded for a time, and in 2005, running as independents, won 20 percent of parliamentary seats. However, since that time, the regime has gone to great lengths to weaken the Brotherhood and hinder its ability to achieve electoral successes. In the November 2010 parliamentary elections, only one Brotherhood candidate (out of about 130 running) won a seat, prompting the organization to join other opposition groups—which, together only won a handful of seats—in boycotting the run-off session as well as the new parliament altogether. This led to a situation where the ruling National Democratic Party (NDP) controlled 90 percent of the seats in parliament.[21]

The other opposition parties in Egypt have had legal status but are small and ineffective. Some analysts have described them as little more than debating societies for Egyptian intellectuals. The most prominent of these parties is the Wafd, a liberal-nationalist party that has a storied past (leading the country to nominal independence against the British in 1922), but is now only a figment of its former self. Others include the liberal Ghad party, led by political dissident Ayman

Nour; the Tagammu party, which espouses a Marxist-type philosophy; and even a Nasserist party, which harkens back to the bygone days of the 1950s and 1960s. The Egyptian government did all it could to keep these parties weak and off-balance. It fomented divisions within these parties[22] and prevented them from boosting their following through certain laws (emergency and otherwise).[23] The government did allow these parties and the Brotherhood to vent publicly, but this was done largely as a safety-valve (letting them blow off steam) and to show Egyptians and the outside world that the country has a semblance of democracy.

The real power in Egypt rested with the presidency, backed by a military and security establishment, and supported by a ruling political party dominated by business interests. The prime minister, Ahmed Nazif, was a U.S.-trained technocrat and an ally of Gamal Mubarak, but he had no independent power base of his own and could be dismissed at any juncture by the president.

CONSTITUTIONAL RULES, CHANGES, AND PROCEDURES

Under the Egyptian Constitution, there must be presidential elections every 6 years. Prior to 2005, Egypt's lower house of parliament, the People's Assembly, would meet to select a candidate by a two-thirds majority, and that candidate would then go before the people in a public referendum (in a yes or no vote) to decide the president. Given the authoritarian nature of the Egyptian regime, with the ruling party beholden to the president and this party in charge of parliament, there was never any doubt that the sitting president, running for another term in office, would be re-elected. In the spring of 2005, bowing to pressure from Egyptian democracy activists and the Bush administration, President Mubarak decided to amend the constitution (which was subsequently passed by a public referendum) that would allow the presidential election to be contested between leaders of legal political parties, provided that such parties have representation in parliament. The latter provision was waved in 2005 because only a handful of opposition parties had seats in parliament. Under the amended Constitution, an independent candidate could also run if he received 250 signatures from parliamentary and local council members.[24] Given the ruling party's dominance of the Egyptian political system, it is highly unlikely that an independent candidate would be able to muster the necessary signatures to become a candidate. In any event, presidential elections in September 2005 were the first "multi-candidate" elections in Egypt's history. President Hosni Mubarak won with 88 percent of the vote, and political dissident Ayman Nour, head of the Ghad (Tomorrow) party, came in second with 7.6 percent of the vote. Other candidates received lesser percentages.

Prior to the revolution in January and February 2011, many questions had arisen regarding the September 2011 presidential election: Would President Hosni Mubarak run for re-election? Would he step down and allow the ruling NDP to field another candidate? Would this NDP candidate be the president's son, Gamal Mubarak, the Deputy Secretary General of the party and head of the party's influential Policies Secretariat? Would another leader emerge within the party and be the NDP's candidate? And what about the legal opposition parties? The decision of most of these parties to withdraw from parliament (claiming the parliamentary elections of November-December 2010 were rigged) means that, under the Constitution, they would not be able to field a presidential candidate. Would there be another constitutional amendment to allow for broader political contestation of the presidential election, such as allowing candidates of political parties not represented in parliament to run in the election?

SUCCESSION SCENARIOS THROUGH LEGAL MECHANISMS

Scenario #1—Hosni Mubarak decides not to run for re-election and the NDP chooses Gamal Mubarak as its candidate who wins handily in a presidential election.

Many Egyptian political analysts believed this was the most likely scenario, given the former political landscape and Hosni Mubarak's advancing age. For many years, it seemed that Hosni Mubarak had been grooming his second son, Gamal Mubarak, to replace him. Gamal, age 47, an investment banker by profession, has made his mark as a leader within the ruling party. He assumed leadership of the NDP's new Policies Secretariat in 2002, the main policymaking body within the party, and has used this position to modernize the party, shed its socialist legacy, and adopt a more free-market orientation.[25] Gamal has placed many of his allies in the party in the Policies Secretariat, including multi-millionaires like Ahmed Ezz, a steel magnate, and Mohamed Kamal, a U.S.-trained political scientist. President Mubarak has also taken Gamal on official trips with him abroad, including to

Washington, adding fuel to the speculation that a father-to-son transition is in the works. Although Gamal has denied that he was seeking the presidency as late as November 2010,[26] few in Egypt believe him. There were also unofficial campaigns within the NDP for Gamal to run for president, as well as a poster campaign (with supporters plastering his image on walls in Cairo) for the same purpose.[27] Given the authoritarian nature of the Egyptian regime, such an "unofficial" campaign could not have taken place without the president's approval. With the NDP having a virtual monopoly on politics in Egypt and with the regime's security apparatus behind him (as directed by the father), there would have been little doubt that Gamal would have won a presidential election under those circumstances.

There are, however, some political observers who say that such a presidential succession was not a foregone conclusion. They point to some liabilities on Gamal's part. For one, outside of his coterie of political allies and businessmen, Gamal was not well-liked by the majority of Egyptian citizens who are struggling to make ends meet amidst growing economic hardships, such as the rise in food prices. In late September 2010, for example, hundreds of demonstrators gathered in Abdeen Square in Cairo to protest against a possible succession of Gamal to the presidency before being cracked down upon by security police.[28] Although the demonstration was organized by opposition groups like the April 6 Youth Movement and Kifaya (Enough), which had an axe to grind, they may have reflected broader public sentiment. And while Gamal has the ability to make good speeches on the need to boost Egyptian incomes, many Egyptians see him and his millionaire-politician allies as being divorced from their own harsh economic realities. Second, there apparently was a leadership rivalry within the NDP, between the old guard (many of whom are in their 70s) who grew up under the socialist policies of Gamal Abdel Nasser and who favor the public sector, and the new guard who want to shrink the public sector and make Egypt even more business-friendly than it currently is. The old guard remained influential within the party, though not as much as it once was. They realized that they could not mount an effective campaign against Gamal as long as Hosni Mubarak remained president, and if the latter had decided not to run for re-election and gave the nod to his son to be his successor, then they would have had to swallow what they saw as a bitter pill. On the other hand, if Gamal's popularity had remained low with the Egyptian people and Hosni Mubarak equivocated about Gamal's political future, then the old guard might have believed they had a chance to sideline Gamal. Third, and perhaps most importantly, rumors were rife in Cairo that Gamal was not well-liked by the military, not helped by the fact that he never did military service and hence is not considered "one of them."[29] Some retired military officers even circulated an open letter in August 2010 criticizing Gamal's potential candidacy for president, and several retired military officers told a *New York Times* correspondent that they were skeptical of "hereditary succession."[30] There were also rumors that, because of this sentiment, Hosni Mubarak cashiered or moved around military officers known to harbor negative views toward his son, and that Gamal himself cultivated some influential officers.[31] Without the military's support, Gamal would have had a difficult time governing the country.

These important liabilities notwithstanding, if Hosni Mubarak had decided that Gamal should be his successor, and he had been healthy enough in office to orchestrate this scenario, then the military establishment and the ruling party would have, in all likelihood, supported his decision. To do otherwise would have jeopardized their own careers and those of their families. Gamal was probably politically-attuned enough to realize that if he had become the NDP's presidential candidate, he would have needed to reach out to the military (assuring them that he would protect their perquisites, economic interests, and autonomy), and to reassure those dependent on the public sector that their social safety net would not be abandoned while he favored his free-market allies.

Scenario #2—Hosni Mubarak decides to run for re-election in 2011, wins handily, but dies in office before he completes his new term.

This scenario stood as good a chance of occurring as the previous scenario. Leading figures in the NDP, as recently as October 2010, have stated that, indeed, Hosni Mubarak would run again in 2011. Whether this comment was made to dampen speculation and controversy about Gamal's potential bid for the presidency or whether it reflected Hosni Mubarak's own inclination is unclear. The elder Mubarak did state publicly a few years ago that he planned to remain president "until his dying breath."[32]

Given his health problems and his advanced age, why would Hosni Mubarak have wanted to run again for president? One reason was that he may have believed the political landscape in Egypt was not ready for a father-to-son transition, especially given the uncertainty about the military's attitude toward Gamal as well as that of the old guard within the NDP. He also may have believed that Gamal himself was not ready to take on the presidency. It is one thing to be in a leadership position of a political party; it is another to be the ruler of a country of some 85 million people. Hosni Mubarak may also have been concerned about his legacy. He was very sensitive to the charges that Egypt was returning to a monarchy—put forth by his and Gamal's detractors—and he threw a prominent dissident, Saad Eddin Ibrahim, in jail for suggesting in an article that Egypt was becoming another Syria (meaning that Hosni Mubarak, like Hafez Asad of Syria, was grooming his son to take over in a "republican" regime). Furthermore, continuing in office might have been considered the least risky path to follow. The Egyptian people, while disgruntled, saw Hosni Mubarak as a known leader who is backed by strong security services. Toying with the unknown, especially at a time of economic unrest—there were hundreds of strikes by workers and professionals over the past few years[33]—might have plunged Egypt and its elite down a path that is full of uncertainties. Hosni Mubarak knows, of course, that his time on earth is limited, but putting off what could be a difficult decision (whether or not to give the nod to Gamal) might have been the least risky decision in his mind over the short term. It should also be remembered that Hosni Mubarak has always been risk averse, a stark contrast to his predecessor, Anwar Sadat, who once famously quipped, "I prefer action to reaction."[34]

In this scenario, after easily winning re-election, Hosni Mubarak would be 83 years old. Given his health problems, there is a strong likelihood that he would die in office because it is difficult to see him lasting until age 89. If succession followed Constitutional procedures in case of the death of the president, the speaker of Egypt's parliament would rule for 60 days, during which presidential candidates from the legal parties *and* those with representation in parliament would campaign, and a leader would be chosen by the people in a popular vote. Under this scenario, the military and security services would not intervene directly in the political system but their leaders would probably meet behind closed doors with the leaders of the NDP to choose the NDP's presidential candidate. It is unlikely that the military and security services would be bystanders in the NDP's candidate selection process, but for the sake of supporting the Egyptian Constitution and legal mechanisms, they would allow the NDP leaders to "formally" choose their leader under party rules after the anointed candidate was selected in a "smoke-filled room."

In this scenario, the military would have an unofficial veto power over the NDP candidate. Given their reported lukewarm or uneasy feelings about Gamal, it is possible, under this scenario, that they would opt for another leader within the NDP to be the presidential candidate. A name that was sometimes floated is 69-year old Ahmed Shafiq, a former air force commander and a hero of the 1973 war, who has been minister of civil aviation since 2002. He was close to Hosni Mubarak (indeed, was a fighter pilot under Mubarak's command when Mubarak was air force commander in 1973) and retired from the military with the rank of lieutenant general.[35] Although he is technically not a leader or a member of a "higher committee" of the NDP, the powers-that-be could have used the fact that he was a cabinet minister to stretch the Constitution a bit to claim that, as a minister, he meets the constitutional requirements. If, in the confines of the closed-door room, the Egyptian military insisted on a particular candidate like Shafiq, it is hard to imagine that NDP leaders would oppose them, since the military has the coercive power in society. The military might also have figured that it could count on the NDP old guard for support since this faction of the party would oppose a Gamal presidency. Given that the presumed candidate would have had the support of the NDP party apparatus and the military, it is likely that this candidate (or another of similar background) would have won easily in a presidential election. The military would have been content that "one of their own"—though now a civilian—would be in charge. Shafiq has the reputation as a no-nonsense administrator. He has been known as a tough boss and was quoted in the Egyptian press in 2005 as stating, "I used to hear my colleagues say this about me, but I am not angry with them. I have lots of friends, and they know that I do not tolerate mistakes for the sake of friendship."[36]

EXTRA-LEGAL SCENARIO SUCCESSIONS

Egyptians pride themselves by living in a country where the rule of law is generally adhered to (even though the law is sometimes not applied in the interest of the ruling apparatus), and thus following Constitutional requirements gives the political system a semblance of legitimacy. Because of this, the legal succession scenarios are more likely than extra-legal ones. Nonetheless, one can envision several scenarios where the powers-that-be in Egypt would sidestep or set aside the Constitution (even if only for a short period of time) in order to preserve what they would see as social stability and the preservation of their perquisites.

Scenario #3—President Hosni Mubarak dies in office and Director of General Intelligence, Omar Soliman, takes over as an interim president for a year.

This scenario would have been unprecedented in Egypt—no Egyptian president has come out of the intelligence services—but it has been the subject of much discussion among the Egyptian intelligentsia. Omar Soliman is considered one of President Mubarak's most trusted advisors. A career military officer, he became head of the powerful Egyptian General Intelligence (EGI) service in 1994 and has remained in this position ever since. EGI played a prominent role in foreign and domestic intelligence, and Mubarak used Soliman on a number of sensitive foreign assignments, such as being an intermediary at times between the Israelis and the Palestinian leadership and as a mediator between the Palestinian factions of Fatah and Hamas.[37] Mubarak also sent Soliman on many trips to Africa and Washington, DC, where he is a well-known interlocutor to the U.S. intelligence community.

Soliman, as an active military officer, could not be a member of the ruling NDP because the Constitution prohibits military officers from being members of political parties. Hence, if Mubarak suddenly died in office, and this scenario played out, Soliman would have had to assume power by extra-legal means.

One subset of this scenario envisions an Omar Soliman-Gamal Mubarak alliance, with the former assuming the role of president while the latter becomes prime minister. This would have given time for Gamal to consolidate his power and reassure the Egyptian military establishment that he would have protected their autonomy, perquisites, and economic interests. The older Soliman (born in 1935 and has some health problems) would then have stepped down after about a year, handing the presidency to Gamal. Shortly before this hand-over, the Constitution would then have been amended to allow for an election by popular vote to give the handover a semblance of legitimacy.

Another subset of this scenario is that Omar Soliman would become president with the backing of the military establishment, effectively sidelining Gamal Mubarak. Soliman would rule for a year and then arrange for other political candidates (not Gamal) to run for president. The preferred presidential candidate would have been an NDP figure who had the support of the military or it could have even been a legal opposition leader (such as from the liberal Wafd party) who reached a *modus vivendi* with the military. Interestingly, some Egyptian political reformers and dissidents were said to favor this scenario because they believed it would be preferable to a dynastic succession of Hosni Mubarak passing power to his son. One Egyptian political liberal stated in the press that she hoped a "patriotic figure from the army will see the unfairness of the system and set things right."[38] Even though it is not clear that the extra-legal scenario of having Soliman at the helm would have led to a democratic Egypt, some members of the intelligentsia were so strongly opposed to dynastic succession that they were presumably willing to take this risk. Curiously, in the summer of 2010, when posters of Gamal Mubarak began appearing on walls and billboards in Cairo touting his credentials as a possible president, posters (though fewer in number) of Omar Soliman also began appearing but were then removed after a few days.[39] Given Soliman's sharp political instincts, it is doubtful that he himself was behind the poster campaign. More likely, the Soliman posters may have been put up by those within the NDP (or others) who are opposed to Gamal's possible presidential ambitions.

Scenario #4—Hosni Mubarak dies in office with no vice president, the NDP is split, rioting takes place in the streets over economic issues, and the military establishment takes over temporarily to restore order, led by Defense Minister Mohammed Tantawi.

This scenario envisions a military coup, albeit one that would eventually hand power back to civilians. Although the military is not eager to rule directly, circumstances might arise where they would see such a temporary take over as being in Egypt's national interests, especially if the social order breaks down or is severely threatened. While Egypt has long been a stable country, there have been times in its recent history, as mentioned earlier, where social strains threatened the stability of the country—most notably the bread riots of 1977 and the police conscript riots of 1986—and the military was called in to restore order when the police proved to be ineffective. A succession crisis by itself would not have necessarily led the military to intervene, but given the economic strains faced by average Egyptian families, some unforeseen event during such a succession crisis might trigger a public uprising or widespread rioting. If the military leaders believe that the country is faced with chaos, they will feel compelled to intervene.

Tantawi, by virtue of his position as Minister of Defense and Field Marshal, is the top military official in the country. As such, he could not be ruled out as a possible successor to Hosni Mubarak during such a scenario, especially if there was no clearly designated successor, such as a vice president. Tantawi commands the entire defense establishment (his full title is Minister of Defense and Military Production and Commander in Chief of the Armed Forces). In the rumor mills of Cairo, however, he was usually not mentioned as one of the top contenders for the presidency. This is because he lacks the charisma and shrewdness of an Omar Soliman, was chosen as defense minister probably because he lacks political ambitions, and was never one to outshine the president. Mubarak clearly wanted someone to lead the military who was the opposite of charismatic Field Marshal Abu Ghazala, a rival of Mubarak's who was forced to retire in 1989.[40] (There was a short-term minister of defense, Lieutenant General Abu Taleb, from 1989 to 1991, at which time Tantawi was named to that position). Tantawi, born in 1935, is a career military officer who served in the 1956, 1967, and 1973 wars, as well as the Gulf War of 1991. Except for certain ceremonial functions, Tantawi has not been in the public eye. If he were to take over in a military coup, he would probably not want to rule for long, and given his age (75), there would be a good possibility that he would move fairly quickly to reestablish civilian rule by choosing or acquiescing to a political leader who would safeguard the military's interests. He would not likely be the sole decisionmaker in this process.

The Egyptian military has the coercive power to bring order to the country (putting tanks and troops into the streets of Cairo and other cities), but the question arises as to what they would do next. The military had no experience in governing for many decades—the Nasser period was more than 40 years ago—and given Egypt's myriad of economic problems would see such a takeover as bringing it numerous headaches and heartaches.[41] Furthermore, given the Egyptian people's preference for the rule of law, the military would not want to be tarnished with taking what would undoubtedly be seen as an undemocratic move. Moreover, a military coup would likely bring criticism from certain circles in the United States and the European Union, possibly jeopardizing military assistance and arms sales. Hence, for a variety of reasons, a military take-over would likely be of relatively short duration.

Scenario #5—Hosni Mubarak dies in office, the NDP cannot decide on a candidate, and the Constitution is set aside to allow Amre Moussa, the former Egyptian foreign minister and current Secretary-General of the Arab League, to run for president with the backing of the military establishment.

Although this scenario may have seemed implausible, given the fact that Moussa is not a politician nor a military officer, in October 2009, he did suggest publicly that he might be interested in running for president some day. He was quoted as saying in an interview with the independent *Shorouk* daily that it was still too soon to decide about standing as a candidate for the presidential election in 2011 but said he appreciated the "trust expressed by many citizens when they talk of my nomination for the presidency . . . and it is a message that has reached me." He added that he was "among the firmest believers in the need to awaken a project for an Egyptian renaissance."[42] Moussa is a charismatic figure who was a very popular foreign minister in the 1990s—so popular, in fact that, as the rumor went, President Mubarak decided to "kick him upstairs" to the position of Secretary-General of the Arab League because, as a cabinet minister, he was overshadowing the president. As foreign minister, Moussa often stood up to Israel and the United States and emphasized Egypt's leadership in the Arab world, positions that won him a supportive following not just in Egypt, but in the larger region. Indicative of his charisma, when Moussa would walk into hotel lobbies in Cairo in the 1990s, the people—mostly a mixture of Egyptians and other Arabs—would start applauding spontaneously.[43]

Moussa is a career diplomat and not a military man, but he is likely to have earned the respect of the Egyptian military establishment when he was foreign minister. In particular, his focus on Israel's reported nuclear arsenal and the perceived threat it posed to Egyptian and regional security was probably appreciated by Egypt's military which, while not wanting to scuttle the peace treaty with Israel, has been traditionally uneasy with the fact that the United States has strongly backed Israel's position of military superiority in the region. While Moussa may still retain the goodwill of the Egyptian military establishment, some high-ranking military officers may fear that he would be too willing to distance Egypt from the United States to the point of jeopardizing critical U.S. military assistance. At the same time, some elements of the Egyptian military, like President Mubarak, might be jealous of Moussa's popularity with the intelligentsia and the masses, and not want such a person as president who would derive his power not from the military establishment but from the public, thus making him less beholden to the military and perhaps less willing to protect their economic interests.

Moussa had not commented publicly about his presumed presidential ambitions since the autumn of 2009 (perhaps not wanting to appear to be too ambitious or not wanting to anger the Mubarak family, which still controls the power in Egypt), but his popularity and his nationalist credentials would have made him a viable contender if the NDP and the military could not decide on an immediate successor. Because Moussa, as Secretary General of the Arab League, does not meet the presidential candidate requirements (being in the leadership of a legal party for at least a year), the Constitution would have had to be amended or set aside for him to have run for office.

Scenario #6—Hosni Mubarak dies in office, the NDP is split, widespread rioting occurs against the regime, the people demand that Muhammad El-Baradei (the former chairman of the International Atomic Energy Agency [IAEA]) become president, the military agrees to allow new elections (with El-Baradei on the ballot), and El-Baradei wins the presidency.

Mohammad El-Baradei, a career Egyptian diplomat, made his mark on the world stage as chairman of the IAEA, especially during the time frame leading up to the Iraq War of 2003 when he defied the Bush administration's assessment of weapons of mass destruction (WMD) in Iraq. After leaving the IAEA El-Baradei returned to Egypt in late 2009 as a national hero but, much to the chagrin of the Egyptian regime, called for the establishment of specific democratic reforms in February 2010. Seeing him as a threat, the Egyptian regime, mainly through its establishment press, sought to malign El-Baradei, but that did not stop him from creating an organization called the National Association for Change. In cooperation with some oppositionists, including members of the Muslim Brotherhood, El-Baradei's followers, as of December 2010, were able to muster close to 1 million Egyptian citizens to sign a petition demanding these democratic changes. Many young Egyptian intellectuals in particular flocked to El-Baradei for a time, seeing him as a sort of savior.[44] El-Baradei, however, has spent much of his time in recent months outside of Egypt, causing some members of the intelligentsia to question his sincerity and seriousness. He urged his followers to boycott the November 2010 parliamentary elections, saying they were going to be a sham because the government had not taken any actions to implement his called-for democratic reforms. Given that the elections turned out as

El-Baradei had predicted, and that most of the opposition parties are boycotting parliament (and even setting up a makeshift shadow parliament), El-Baradei's popularity may be rising again.[45]

What is unclear in this scenario is the military's attitude toward El-Baradei. Some high-ranking military officers may see him as a man of stature who would be more acceptable than Gamal Mubarak, while others may view him warily because of his tacit alliance with the Muslim Brotherhood, even though El-Baradei himself is a secular-liberal. Because El-Baradei is not a leader of a legal political party, he would not have been able to run for president in September 2011 under the Constitution. But, if Hosni Mubarak had died in office and there was no clear successor and if social instability had occurred, the military and security forces might have allowed presidential elections to occur with El-Baradei on the ballot as a way of calming the population. If the NDP split and elections were free and fair, there is a good chance that, under these conditions, El-Baradei might win. However, as the price for allowing him to participate in presidential elections, El Baradei would have had to come to an understanding with the military that if he were to win, he would protect their autonomy, perquisites, and economic interests.

This scenario would have been unlikely because so many events would have had to occur before El-Baradei could have gotten his name on the presidential ballot, but it would not have been beyond the realm of possibility.

Scenario #7—Hosni Mubarak dies in office, the NDP and the military establishment is split, rioting takes place in the streets over economic issues, and the Muslim Brotherhood makes a bid for power and takes over with the support of some military elements.

This would have been the most alarming scenario for the United States (and for countries like Israel) because a Brotherhood-dominated government might scuttle Egypt's peace treaty with Israel, open up the border with Gaza, allow arms to flow to its ideological cousin, Hamas, and spur on other radical fundamentalist movements in the region. The only way this scenario would have occurred is if the Egyptian military, not just the NDP, factionalized, and some elements of the military threw their weight to the Brotherhood. While the Egyptian military is seen as a bastion of the establishment (supporting the nationalist-republican regime that was founded in 1952), and most of its elements are opposed to the Brotherhood—one retired army general said recently that the army would step in with force to prevent the Brotherhood from gaining power—it has not been so obsessed with preserving secularism as has the Turkish military since the time of Kemal Ataturk. Indeed, one of the original Free Officers, Anwar Sadat, outwardly displayed his religiosity as president, released Muslim Brotherhood leaders and activists from prison, and encouraged the formation of Islamic student groups on university campuses as a counterweight to the secular-leftists. In addition, the Egyptian military officer corps in many respects reflects the ideological currents of the Egyptian middle class, which has become more religiously observant and conservative over the past several decades. For example, many wives and daughters of Egyptian military officers wear the *hegab* or headscarf.[46] The military also has built mosques at Egyptian military bases primarily to inculcate conscripts with moderate, establishment Islam as opposed to a more radicalized version of the militant and fundamentalist groups, but in doing so has signaled that religious observance is to be encouraged.[47] Indeed, many, if not most, Egyptian military officers observe the daylight hours of fasting during the month of Ramadan.

There also have been instances where the Egyptian military has even been infiltrated by radical Islamists. President Sadat was assassinated by radical Egyptian Islamic Jihad operatives who were members of the Egyptian military. Although since that time (1981) there have been great efforts to weed out Islamist elements from the military, it is conceivable that some junior officers may harbor sympathetic sentiments toward nonviolent but fundamentalist groups like the Muslim Brotherhood.

Under this scenario, the Brotherhood itself would have had to change its position and tactics. Although it once had a violent and secret wing (especially in the 1940s and 1950s—assassinating some regime figures such as Prime Minister Al-Nuqrashi Pasha in 1948), since the 1970s it has renounced violence and sought to participate in the political process.[48] It has also concentrated on pursuing the gradual Islamization of Egyptian society, abetted by its extensive social-charitable network. The Egyptian government, especially under Hosni Mubarak, has not trusted the Brotherhood, and has steadfastly kept the Brotherhood in legal limbo. Although the Brotherhood has been able to field parliamentary candidates in recent elections, running as independents, the fact that the Brotherhood remains an illegal organization allowed the government to conduct periodic roundups of hundreds of Brotherhood activists and keep them in prison, sometimes for months, if not years, at a time. Despite this continual harassment and persecution, the leadership of the Brotherhood instructed its followers not to resist and to be patient, most likely under the philosophy that politics would follow society—in other words, what is important is for Egyptian society to become more devout and follow Islamic precepts. When Islamization of society reaches a critical mass, then a truly Islamic state, led by leaders devoted to implementing the *sharia* (Islamic law), could be achieved.[49]

At the same time, the Brotherhood, as the largest opposition group in Egypt, has come to believe that they can spur the Islamization process along by getting some of their members elected to parliament. The apex of this "political process" strategy was in 2005 when, for reasons aimed largely at frightening the United States (which put significant pressure on the Egyptian government to democratize), the Egyptian government adopted a liberal policy toward the Brotherhood, releasing members from prison, allowing the organization to campaign openly using religious slogans (which were banned by the Constitution), and even affording the Supreme Guide of the Brotherhood an interview in the semi-official newspaper, *Al-Ahram*. The aim of the Egyptian government was to squeeze the secular-liberal opposition and allow some Brotherhood gains to present the United States with a picture of either "us" (meaning the Mubarak government and the ruling NDP) or "them" (meaning the fundamentalist Brotherhood). Things did not go exactly as planned because the Brotherhood did better than expected in the first round of the elections (parliamentary elections then were held in three rounds and run-offs during a 6-week period), and the NDP did more poorly than expected. The Brotherhood then mobilized its members to score even bigger gains, which sent the government into panic mode. Thereafter, the government tried its best to rig subsequent rounds of the election and suppress the vote, but the Brotherhood wound up capturing 20 percent of parliamentary seats, the largest ever recorded by the organization in Egypt.

Although the Brotherhood's significant gains in Egypt between 2000 and 2005 (going from 17 to 88 seats), along with the Hamas victory in the Palestinian territories, appeared to have dampened the Bush administration's push for democratization in the Arab world,[50] the Egyptian government signaled that it would not allow a repeat of such a Brotherhood victory. In the days up to the 2010 parliamentary elections, it arrested hundreds of Brotherhood activists and ensured that most Brotherhood candidates were not elected; indeed, only one Brotherhood candidate (out of about 130 who ran) won a seat in the first round of the elections, prompting the Brotherhood, along with most of the other opposition parties, to boycott the run-off round and refuse to participate in the new parliament.[51]

The Brotherhood's experiment with political participation thus has proven to be a tough row to hoe. Although there is no evidence that the Brotherhood has given up on its nonviolent strategy, it is not a monolithic organization. Indeed, its decision to participate in the 2010 parliamentary elections was highly controversial within the organization itself, with a substantial minority opposing the decision.[52] The Brotherhood has its moderate and more hard-line wings as well as generational differences. Although it would have much to lose if it were to change strategies and revert to a militant role (as it did in the 1940s and 1950s), it is not inconceivable that some members of its more hard-line faction may have opted for such a change, especially if they believed that dissatisfaction with the government by the people was so profound that they believed violent change was coming and they might as well take advantage of the situation.

This scenario envisions widespread rioting and violence by the people over economic conditions (perhaps because of price increases) and a breakdown of order. Hard-line elements of the Brotherhood come to believe that the moment is ripe to make a bid for power, essentially giving up on the gradual approach of the past few decades. These hard-line elements take leadership of the rioters and make overtures to the military, which believes it can only restore order if it bows to the will of the people. The Brotherhood is allowed to take power with the support of key factions of the military who assure the people that this will be a popular regime that is not only Islamic in its orientation but geared toward improving the lot of the poor. The military senses that its own interests would be threatened if it did not back such a movement. A *modus vivendi* of sorts is established, where a more outwardly Islamist-oriented military rules behind the scenes, while the Brotherhood declares Egypt an Islamic republic. Elections are held to legitimize the Brotherhood in power. The Brotherhood then takes the political decision to end Egypt's peace treaty with Israel, ends the close security cooperation with the United States, and reaches out to other Islamist groups in the Middle East like Hamas and Hezbollah (even though the latter is a Shiite organization). The United States loses its military cooperation with the Egyptian government as more Islamic-oriented officers take over the leadership of the military and pro-Western military officers are purged from the ranks. Although this new Egyptian regime would not likely initiate a war against Israel (unsure of the outcome), it could pursue certain policies that might trigger an Israeli military response. For example, it could send large numbers of troops and military equipment into the Sinai in violation of the peace treaty with Israel and provide military assistance to Hamas. Israel, believing its national security is at stake, would then reoccupy the Gaza Strip and invade the Sinai, leading to a new Arab-Israeli war.

HOW WOULD THESE SCENARIOS IMPACT U.S.-EGYPTIAN RELATIONS?

Legal Succession Scenarios.

Scenario #1—If Hosni Mubarak decided not to run in 2011 and Gamal Mubarak ran and won the presidential election, the substance of U.S.-Egyptian strategic ties would have been largely unaffected. To bolster his own legitimacy, however, Gamal might have taken certain steps to show that he is a nationalist leader and not simply a toady of the United States. He might have outwardly taken some positions in the Arab-Israeli peace process or on regional issues (like Iran) that would appear to be counter to U.S. policy goals. But as the son of Hosni Mubarak and from the Westernized elite of the country, Gamal would likely continue the close political and strategic relationship with the United States. Moreover, as someone who did not do military service, and given his problematic standing (at best) with the Egyptian military establishment, Gamal would also not want to harm the U.S. military aid spigot that the Egyptian military has relied on for decades.

Scenario #2—Hosni Mubarak dies in office before he designates a successor, and the NDP and the military and security services meet behind closed doors to chose a presidential candidate who would be acceptable to the power structure in the country. Under this scenario, the basic structure of the regime remains in place, with the speaker of parliament ruling temporarily for 60 days before a presidential election can take place. The NDP and military elite decide on a candidate behind closed doors. Whether it would have been a former military officer and current cabinet minister like Ahmed Shafik, Gamal Mubarak, or another NDP figure, the regime would remain in charge. Any of these possible candidates from the NDP would likely win a presidential election, given the NDP's near monopoly of politics in the country, and U.S-Egyptian strategic relations would likely be unaffected in any major way. In some respects, having another establishment NDP figure other than Hosni Mubarak at the helm in Egypt might actually improve the chances for stability because any new leader, even Gamal Mubarak, would see the pursuit of some democratic reforms as important for his own legitimacy,[53] even if these reforms are not very dramatic. Such reforms would likely be welcomed by the U.S. administration and Congress, and could even lead to a warming of the bilateral relationship. On December 18, 2010, U.S. Assistant Secretary of State for Democracy, Human Rights, and Labor Michael Posner wrote: "It is the [Obama] administration's firm view that progress in political and economic reform in Egypt is essential to the country's long-term strength and success as a regional leader as well as to sustaining a strong foundation for our valued strategic partnership."[54]

Extra-Legal Scenarios.

Scenario #3—Under this scenario, Hosni Mubarak dies in office and Egyptian General Intelligence

Director Omar Soliman takes power for a year—the U.S.-Egyptian strategic partnership would also be maintained. Soliman, as a well-known interlocutor with U.S. military and intelligence agencies, understands the importance of maintaining close security ties with the United States for Egypt's own national security and will probably keep these ties on an even keel. However, if this scenario had come to pass, Soliman would be sidestepping the Egyptian Constitution because he would assume the presidency in extra-legal ways. This might elicit criticism within the human rights and democracy advocate communities not only in Egypt, but in Washington and other western capitals—even though some Egyptian democracy activists claim they would favor this outcome because it would forestall a Gamal presidency.[55] Hence, there would likely have been calls from some U.S. Congress members to cut aid to Egypt if civilian rule via presidential elections, and all aspects of the Egyptian Constitution, were not restored in a short period of time. Much would depend on how Soliman mitigated this criticism by emphasizing the temporary nature of his rule and outlining his plans for elections of a civilian president. If skeptics in Congress can be convinced that he is sincere about the temporary nature of the coup and believe that an alternative at that point might have produced a shakier outcome, then punitive measures—like cutting U.S. military aid—would be minimized. On the other hand, should Soliman not step down after a year and not move forward to restore Constitutional mechanisms, events could be set in motion that could harm U.S.-Egyptian strategic ties. In other words, if Soliman were to overstay his leadership, and the United States were to show its displeasure by threatening or indeed cutting aid, then U.S.-Egyptian relations would likely suffer.

Scenario #4—This scenario—the Egyptian military takes power temporarily in response to widespread social unrest, with Defense Minister Tantawi in charge—is similar to the previous scenario, but it might actually have been more palatable to the Egyptian intelligentsia and to Washington because the coup could be seen as a necessary measure to forestall chaos. The Egyptian military could mitigate the political fallout by reassuring both audiences that it wants to hand back authority to civilians, by scheduling a presidential election as soon as possible, and by crafting democratic reforms to allow for freer and fairer elections than have occurred so far in Egypt. Tantawi and other members of the Egyptian military hierarchy would probably see the continuation of U.S.-Egyptian strategic ties as important for their country's stability, but if social unrest were not to end and the Egyptian military were to use U.S. military armaments to cause bloodshed on the streets for a considerable period of time, there would likely be calls from the U.S. Congress and parts of the U.S. administration to cut military aid to Egypt, thus jeopardizing the security relationship. Hence, much would depend on how quickly the Egyptian military would be able to restore order and how quickly they would be able to hold civilian elections and make the transition back to civilian rule.

Scenario #5—If the NDP were to split and the military agreed to sidestep the Constitution to allow Amre Moussa to run and win the presidency, the regime might initially have more legitimacy and popularity because Moussa would play to Egyptian nationalist sentiments and might allow for some democratic reforms. Moussa would be more willing to challenge U.S. policies in the region, particularly over Arab-Israeli issues and possibly over Iran, but as a longtime member of the Egyptian establishment, he would not want to alienate the Egyptian military by causing severe tensions with the United States to the point where the United States starts to question Egypt as a strategic partner. One could expect Moussa, despite wanting to show differences with the United States over some foreign policy issues, to continue close U.S.-Egyptian military and security ties, especially as those are largely out of the public spotlight.

Scenario #6—Under this scenario—where El-Baradei would be elected president through splits in the NDP and the military agreeing to set aside parts of the Constitution—U.S.-Egyptian strategic ties would likely follow a pattern similar to that of Scenario #4. El Baradei would probably take some foreign policy positions at variance with the United States not only because of his own troubled history with U.S. policy, but because doing so would bolster his legitimacy at home. At the same time, understanding that he could not have been allowed to run for president without the support of the military establishment, he would be mindful not to make his differences with the United States so profound that they would wind up hurting U.S.-Egyptian military and security ties. Hence, like the Amre Moussa scenario, El Baradei would likely continue the close U.S.-Egyptian strategic ties, especially since they are mostly out of the public spotlight.

Scenario #7—This scenario would be the most alarming for U.S.-Egyptian strategic relations because a Brotherhood-dominated regime would likely scuttle the Egyptian-Israeli peace treaty, aid Hamas, and lessen, if not end, military ties with the United States. Although there may be more moderate elements of the Brotherhood who would want to take a measured approach to these issues, this scenario envisions hard line elements of the organization taking over. The United States military would likely lose its over-flight and transit rights through the Suez Canal, and joint military exercises would end. In addition, cooperation on anti-terrorism would end because the Brotherhood would not want to be seen aiding the U.S. fight against Islamists, even though the Brotherhood would likely remain opposed to Al Qaeda. One mitigating factor would be the Egyptian military. Although this scenario envisions a purging of the military, the Brotherhood would not want to emasculate it because the Brotherhood would see the military as important for a possible confrontation with Israel. Some of the remaining elements of the Egyptian military, even those with Islamist sympathies, would be wary of ending the U.S. military assistance program entirely, especially since the Egyptian military relies heavily on U.S. military equipment. However, certain dynamics would likely come into play if a Brotherhood-dominated regime were to come to power in Egypt, namely that the U.S. Congress would be hard-pressed to continue funding military aid to Egypt if the Brotherhood were to take power.

POLICY RECOMMENDATIONS

How Should U.S. Officials Conduct Themselves in These Scenarios?

As the events of the past few months have shown us, the transtition of Egyptian leadership happened based on events and processes inside Egypt, and the United States and other powers (Isreal, Saudi Arabia, and others) had little influence over the outcome.[56] Nonetheless, based on these scenarios, there are some things U.S. policymakers should and should not do during what is currently a very sensitive time in modern Egyptian history.

First, the United States should not signal that it prefers one leader over another. While this monograph has suggested that the end result of certain regime changes would more likely preserve U.S.-Egyptian strategic ties than others, the United States should refrain from speaking publicly about them. The reasons are two-fold. First, with their history of Western domination, Egyptians would react angrily to any perception that the United States was "pulling the strings" about who should lead Egypt. In an episode well-known to educated Egyptians, in February 1942, British tanks surrounded King Farouk's palace and the British Ambassador threatened to start shooting if the king did not appoint a pro-Allied Wafd government. The king relented in what was seen by most Egyptians as an act of national humiliation.[57] Although the British justified their actions because they had their backs to the wall—German and Italian armies were in Egypt's western desert, threatening the major cities of Alexandria and Cairo and the vital Suez Canal—to Egyptians this was an egregious example of foreign and imperial domination. Any suggestion by the United States that it would prefer a particular candidate would likely backfire.

Second, U.S. officials should be mindful that long-term U.S.-Egyptian interests require not only the assent of the political-military establishment but the population as well, or more specifically, at least the educated strata in Egyptian society who want their country to be more democratic. U.S. officials should speak not only about the desirability of the Egyptian government adhering to Egyptian Constitutional procedures during any period of regime change, but allowing more freedoms and rights for political parties to contest elections in a more democratic manner. Indeed, this approach has already begun with an op-ed piece in the *Washington Post* by a senior State Department official (the Assistant Secretary of State for Democracy, Human Rights, and Labor), who wrote on December 18, 2010:

> Free and fair elections require free and vibrant media; that includes bloggers and international coverage. The Egyptian government could also do more to encourage a broader array of political parties and to support citizens who want to form non-governmental organizations to contribute to the country's future. It will also be important for Egypt to welcome both international and domestic election monitors and allow them to carry out their work freely throughout the campaign period and on [Presidential] Election Day next September [2011].[58]

Even though Hosni Mubarak is no longer in office, similar promouncements can still be made by high-ranking officials to underscore that they come from the top of the U.S. administration.

But now that we face a situation in some ways similar to Scenarios #3 and #4, how should U.S. officials conduct themselves if the Egyptian military takes power, even if only for a short period of time? This is a delicate matter than needs to be handled with some dexterity and much depends on the situation on the ground. If the military steps in to allow popular candidates—who are not in leadership positions of political parties—to run in a contested presidential election and allows such elections to take place in a free and fair manner, then Washington should show some leniency to the sidestepping of the Egyptian Constitution, especially since this Constitution is heavily skewed toward the ruling party. If a popular leader is elected and undertakes reforms that benefit the people and lead to long-term stability, that would be in both countries' strategic interests. And even if such a leader would be more critical of U.S. policies than Hosni Mubarak has been, the new leader would, in all likelihood, want to maintain U.S.-Egyptian strategic ties not only to please the Egyptian military establishment, but to enhance Egypt's national security.

A military coup that would put the military in charge of the country for a period of time would be more problematic because it could lead the relationship down a slippery slope where the U.S. administration would not want to be seen aiding an undemocratic process and the U.S. Congress might feel compelled to apply punitive measures, such as cutting military aid. Indeed, several years ago, Congress withheld $100 million in military aid to Egypt largely because of its undemocratic practices, but it supplied a "national security waiver" to this legislation that was exercised by Secretary of State Condoleezza Rice 2 months later.[59] A military coup would likely lead to even more punitive measures. Nonetheless, if a military coup took place to end widespread civil strife in Egypt, and Egyptian military leaders pledged to restore civilian rule and bring about democratic changes, then U.S. officials should resist punishing Egypt. At the same time, U.S. officials should hold the Egyptian military accountable, and if they do not return to the barracks and restore civilian rule as they promised, then the U.S. administration should take the lead in pressuring the regime with punitive measures. Although such a policy on the part of the United States may seem counterproductive from a strategic point of view, as the

Egypt military might react angrily to such measures, Egyptian military officers would understand that they would be hurting their own security interests if they were to indefinitely postpone civilian elections. While the U.S.-Egyptian strategic relationship would suffer a setback, most likely it would be temporary. U.S. military officers who interact with their Egyptian counterparts would also have a role to play under these scenarios, informing them that the return to civilian rule would be not only desirable from a political point of view but be in the long-term interest of preserving the bilateral security relationship and military assistance levels.

With the exception of a Muslim Brotherhood takeover, whoever becomes the new president of Egypt will likely want to establish a good relationship with Washington. As this new president or leader takes the helm in Cairo, the United States has the opportunity to impress upon him the need to pursue reforms in the interests of the long-term stability of the country. Washington should assure the new leader of its support by pledging that the bilateral security relationship that has been built up over the past 3 decades will continue, and that politically, Washington will also support him, provided that domestic political reforms will indeed be carried out. Washington should also emphasize that rigging of elections, cracking down on opposition media, and arrests of nonviolent opponents not only hurts the country's image overseas but is counterproductive to preserving Egypt's long-term stability.

Finally, if the Muslim Brotherhood takes over and pursues policies that not only weaken or end U.S.-Egyptian strategic ties but assist violent groups in the region, (Scenario #7), the United States should seek to isolate the government and suspend aid to it, hoping that more moderate elements would eventually emerge in Egypt. At the same time, the United States should counsel Israel not to take aggressive policies against Egypt unless it truly believes its national security is directly threatened, as an Israeli-Egyptian war could lead to untold consequences and embolden radicals in the region. Although the prospect of a hostile regime in Egypt would certainly set back U.S. strategic interests in the region, including the chances to achieve an Israeli-Palestinian peace deal as well as a broader Arab-Israeli peace, a hostile Egyptian government would not end the U.S. standing in the region, as the United States would have the option of strengthening its ties to other countries in the area. Losing Egypt as a partner and an ally would undoubtedly be a severe setback for U.S. national security interests, but such a loss would not necessarily be of long duration. Some elements of the Egyptian military, even those who would profess loyalty to a Brotherhood-dominated government, would not want to cut off U.S. ties completely, especially since so much of Egypt's military equipment is U.S.-made, and the Westernized elite of the country would not want to see it move to a sort of pariah status in the international community like that of Iran. U.S. officials, while putting pressure on a Brotherhood-dominated government, should also understand that not all elements of such a government would be inherently hostile to the United States, and while it would be difficult to return to the present era of close U.S.-Egyptian strategic relations, there might be a chance to at least contain such a regime's more hostile ambitions. It should be remembered that the United States had cool-to-hostile relations with Egypt for most of the Nasser period, but eventually a new leader, Sadat, from the same regime, emerged and pursued certain polices that warmed the relationship. In any event, of all the scenarios outlined in this monograph, the radical Brotherhood regime scenario stands the least chance of succeeding because the Egyptian military is likely to hold firm and not split apart, precluding a Brotherhood take-over.

ENDNOTES

1. "Security Assistance: State and DOD Need to Assess How Foreign Military Financing Program for Egypt Achieves U.S. Foreign Policy and Security Goals," *Report to the Committee on International Relations, House of Representatives*, Washington, DC: U.S. Government Accountability Office, April 2006, p. 17.

2. *Ibid.*, pp. 2-18. On Bright Star, see *www.globalsecurity.org/military/ops/bright-star.htm*.

3. Jeffrey Fleishman, "For Egypt, Mubarak's Health and Successor are Guessing Games," *Los Angeles Times*, August 24, 2010.

4. See Michele Dunne, "A Post-Pharaonic Egypt?" *American Interest*, September-October 2008.

5. Roger Owen, *State, Power, and Politics in the Making of the Modern Middle East*, London, UK, and New York: Routledge, 2008, pp. 178-185.

6. Imad Harb, "The Egyptian Military in Politics: Disengagement or Accommodation?" *The Middle East Journal*, Vol. 52, No. 2, Spring 2003, p. 278.

7. *Ibid.*

8. *Ibid.*

9. *Ibid.*, p. 279.

10. *Ibid.*, p. 282.

11. Steven A. Cook, *Ruling But Not Governing: The Military and Political Development in Egypt, Algeria, and Turkey*, Baltimore, MD: Johns Hopkins University Press, 2007, pp. 73-74.

12. Joseph Kechichian and Jeanne Nazimek, "Challenges to the Military in Egypt," Middle East Policy, Vol. V, No. 3, September 1997, p. 128. See also Raymond Hinnebusch, "The Formation of the Contemporary Egyptian State from Nasser and Sadat to Mubarak," in Ibrahim Oweiss, ed., *The Political Economy of Contemporary Egypt*, Washington, DC: Georgetown University Press, 1990, pp. 204-209.

13. Thanassis Cambinis, "Succession Gives Army a Stiff Test in Egypt," *New York Times*, September 11, 2010.

14. Harb, p. 285.

15. Cook, p. 74.

16. Cambinis.

17. Afaf Marsot, "Democratization in Egypt," in Oweiss, ed., p. 292.

18. Stephen Roll, "Gamal Mubarak and the Discord in Egypt's Ruling Elite," *Arab Reform Bulletin*, September 1, 2010. See also Magdi Abdelhadi, "Egyptians look to military 'savior,'" *BBC News*, June 23, 2009.

19. Marwa Hussein, "Businessmen gain more leverage in parliament," *Al-Ahram Online*, December 22, 2010.

20. Cook, pp. 88-92.

21. Michael Slackman, "Egypt's Critics Have a Voice, but Never the Last Word," *New York Times*, February 18, 2009.

22. Amr Hamzawy, "Egypt's Legitimacy Crisis in the Aftermath of Flawed Elections," Washington, DC: Carnegie Endowment for International Peace, December 5, 2010, available from *carnegie-mec.org/publications/?fa=42067&lang=en*.

23. Gregory L. Aftandilian, "Looking Forward. An Integrated Strategy for Supporting Democracy and Human Rights in Egypt," *Project on Middle East Democracy*, May 2009, p. 10, available from *www.pomed.org/aftandilian-egypt-may-2009*. See also Mona El-Nahas, "Pointless Parties," *Al-Ahram Weekly*, January 1-6, 2009; and Slackman, February 19, 2009.

24. See "Egypt's Elections: The Constitutional and Legal Framework," Washington, DC: Carnegie Endowment for International Peace, available from *carnegie-mec.orgpublications/?fa=42067&lang=en*.

25. Stephen Glain, "Egypt After Mubarak," *The Nation*, April 27, 2009.

26. "Gamal Mubarak: I Know Nothing About Campaigns Supporting Me as a Presidential Candidate and I'm not Interested in Them," *Al Shorouk* (in Arabic), November 12, 2010.

27. Available from *www.haaretz.com/news/international/new-poster-campaign-backs-gamal-mubarak-for-egyptian-presidency-1.309522*.

28. Jack Shenker, "Protests in Egypt against Gamal succession plans," *The Guardian*, September 21, 2010. See also Heba Fahmy, "Police clamp down on anti-Gamal Mubarak protestors," September 22, 2010, available from *thedailynewsegypt.com*.

29. Jeffrey Azarva, "Obama and Egypt's Coming Succession Crisis, Middle East Review of International Affairs," December 1, 2008; and Amin Elmasry, "The Myth of Gamal Mubarak," June 26, 2010, available from *aminelmasry.wordpress.com/2010/06/27/the-myth-of-gamal-mubarak/*.

30. Cambinis.

31. Interview with an Egyptian intellectual, March 24, 2010.

32. Adam Shatz, "Mubarak's Last Breath," *London Review of Books*, Vol. 32, No. 20, May 27, 2010.

33. Abigail Hauslohner, "As Egypt's Mubarak Comes to Washington, Labor Unrest Surges," *Time*, August 17, 2009.

34. As quoted in Ali E. Hillal Dessouki, "The Primacy of Economics: the Foreign Policy of Egypt," Baghat Korany and Ali E. Hillal Dessouki, eds., *The Foreign Policies of Arab States*, Boulder, CO, and London, UK: Westview Press, 1984, p. 133.

35. Available from *weekly.ahram.org/eg/print/2005/759/profile.htm*.

36. *Ibid*.

37. Shatz. See also Webster Brooks, "Egypt's Succession Crisis: Mohamed El Baradei and Omar Suleiman Hold the Keys to the Presidency," *Booker Rising*, April 3, 2010.

38. As quoted in Abdelhadi.

39. Available from *www.bbc.co.uk/news/world-middle-east-11169725*.

40. Cook, p. 73.

41. See the comments by one of the few living Free Officers, Tharwat Okasha, in Abdelhadi. See also Tarek Masoud, "Is Gamal Mubarak the best hope for Egyptian democracy?" *Foreign Policy*, September 23, 2010.

42. As quoted in "Egypt needs a renaissance: Arab League chief," Agence-France Press, October 20, 2009.

43. Interview with an Egyptian intellectual, February 9, 2007.

44. Available from *egyptianchronicles.blogspot.com/2010/12/elbaradei-in-upper-egypt-day-1.html*.

45. Asharf Khalil, "Interview: El Baradei on quiet revolution, reform tactics, and religion," *Al Masry Al Youm*, December 23, 2010. See also Amr El-Shobaki, "Parties, Movements, and Prospects for Change in Egypt," *Arab Reform Bulletin*, May 20, 2010.

46. In the 1980s, for example, even the wife of Defense Minister and Field Marshal Abu Ghazala wore the *hegab*. See Cook, p. 87.

47. Stephen Gotowicki, "The Military In Egyptian Society," in Phebe Marr, ed., *Egypt at the Crossroads: Domestic Stability and Regional Role*, Washington, DC: National Defense University Press, 1997, pp. 106-116.

48. Ana Belen Soage and Jorge Fuentelsaz Franganillo, "The Muslim Brothers in Egypt," in Barry Rubin, ed., *The Muslim Brotherhood. The Organization and Policies of a Global Islamist Movement*, New York: Palgrave Macmillan, 2010, pp. 40-41.

49. Gilles Keppel, *Muslim Extremism in Egypt: The Prophet and the Pharaoh*, Berkeley and Los Angeles, CA: University of California Press, 2003, p. 93.

50. Aftandilian, pp. 6-9.

51. Michele Dunne and Amr Hamzawy, "From Too Much Egyptian Opposition to Too Little—and Legal Worries Besides," *Carnegie Commentary*, December 13, 2010. See also "Egyptians Riot, Burn Cars, Claiming Vote Fraud," Associated Press, November 29, 2010.

52. Amr Hamzawy and Michele Dunne, "Brotherhood Enters Elections in a Weakened State," *Carnegie Commentary*, November 15, 2010.

53. See the interesting argument put forward by Tarek Masoud, "Is Gamal Mubarak the best hope for Egyptian democracy?" *Foreign Policy*, September 23, 2010.

54. Michael Posner, "A chance for democracy in Egypt," *Washington Post* op-ed, December 18, 2010.

55. Larbi Sadiki, "Eid Mubarak, Egypt! As Gamal Mubarak seeks his father's throne, will hereditary succession again restrict democratization in an Arab state?" *AlJazeera.net*, November 25, 2010, available from *english.aljazeera.net/indepth/opinion/2010/2010/11/20101123745718188O.html*.

56. See Chuck Freilich, "Inscrutable face of Egypt's future," *Washington Times* op-ed, July 23, 2010.

57. P. J. Vatikiotis, *The Modern History of Egypt*, London, UK: Weidenfeld and Nicholson, 1969, pp. 315-411.

58. Posner.

59. "Ms. Rice's Retreat," *Washington Post* editorial, March 11, 2008.